I Gave At The Office

I GAVE AT THE OFFICE

by Greg Howard and Craig MacIntosh

A SALLY FORTH® Collection

Andrews and McMeel
A Universal Press Syndicate Company
Kansas City

HAVE YOU NOTICED THAT EVERY TIME YOU TURN AROUND THESE DAYS, SOMEONE'S TALKING ABOUT SELF-ESTEEM?

LOOK AT THIS. LOW SELF-ESTEEM IS BEING BLAMED FOR EVERY CONCEIVABLE KIND OF PROBLEM.

THE FLUSH VALVE ON THE TOILET NEEDS FIXING, BUT I'M WAITING TILL I FEEL BETTER ABOUT MYSELF.

NOW YOU'RE BEING SILLY.

CAREFUL, YOU'LL DAMAGE MY SELF-ESTEEM.

MAYBE I'M OLD-FASHIONED, TED, BUT I THINK THEY'RE TAKING THIS SELF-ESTEEM STUFF WAY TOO FAR.

IN WHAT WAY?

IT USE TO BE THAT KIDS LEARNED TO FEEL GOOD ABOUT THEMSELVES BY DOING SOMETHING WORTH FEELING GOOD ABOUT. BUT NOW THEY TELL US TO REWARD KIDS FOR EVERY LITTLE — THING.

I DIDN'T STICK GUM IN MY EAR TODAY. WHEN DO I GET MY TROPHY?

I SEE WHAT YOU MEAN.

ANYTHING NEW AT SCHOOL, HONEY?

MY TEACHER IS STARTING A NEW GRADING SYSTEM. IT'S SUPPOSED TO RAISE OUR STEAM.

SELF-ESTEEM?

YEAH, THAT'S IT. ANYWAY, NOW THE BEST GRADE IS AN "A++++" AND THE WORST GRADE IS AN "A."

I KNEW IT WOULD COME TO THIS.

YOU'RE LOOKING AT AN "A+" STUDENT.

I'M GETTING REALLY TIRED OF ALL THIS DRIVEL ABOUT SELF-ESTEEM. IT'S POPPING UP EVERYWHERE.

DID I TELL YOU I GOT APPOINTED TO THE EMPOWERMENT COMMITTEE AT WORK?

SEE WHAT I MEAN? IT'S EVEN WEASELED ITS WAY WAY INTO THE WORKPLACE.

YOU WOULDN'T GET SO WORKED UP ABOUT STUFF IF YOU HAD MORE SELF-ESTEEM.

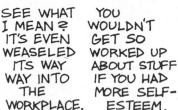

TED...

THE PROBLEM WITH YOU LOW SELF-ESTEEM PEOPLE IS YOU CAN'T TAKE A JOKE.

DO YOU REALIZE WE SPEND BILLIONS OF DOLLARS EVERY YEAR ON PROGRAMS DESIGNED TO RAISE PEOPLE'S SELF-ESTEEM?

IS THAT BAD?

MAYBE NOT, BUT WHAT ABOUT THE PEOPLE WHO ARE A MAJOR PAIN IN THE REAR BECAUSE THEY HAVE **TOO MUCH** SELF-ESTEEM. WHY AREN'T WE SPENDING MONEY ON PROGRAMS TO LOWER THEIRS?

I WORK WITH A LOT OF PEOPLE WHO COULD USE THAT KIND OF HELP, YOU KNOW.

YOU KNOW WHAT I DON'T LIKE ABOUT THIS WHOLE SELF-ESTEEM TREND? I THINK A LOT OF TIMES IT'S JUST A WAY OF PASSING THE BUCK.

WE GO AROUND BLAMING ALL OUR PROBLEMS ON LOW SELF-ESTEEM BECAUSE OF THINGS THAT HAPPENED DECADES AGO. WHY CAN'T WE JUST ACT LIKE ADULTS, TAKE RESPONSIBILITY FOR OUR SHORTCOMINGS AND WORK ON DOING BETTER?

YOU MEAN LIKE ACTUALLY ADMIT SOMETHING IS OUR OWN FAULT? SOUNDS PRETTY UN-AMERICAN TO ME, SAL.

18

MAYBE WE JUST **THINK** WE'RE HAPPY. MAYBE WE NEED TO TAKE A HARDER LOOK TO SEE IF UNDERNEATH THIS HAPPINESS WE'RE ACTUALLY UNHAPPY.

23

ONE OF US IS SUPPOSED TO GO TO THIS SEMINAR... SOMETHING ABOUT NEW WAYS OF DESIGNING OFFICE SPACE TO MAKE EMPLOYEES MORE EFFICIENT.

SOUNDS INTERESTING. I'LL GO.

OKAY, BUT I DON'T WANT YOU COMING BACK WITH A BUNCH OF STUPID IDEAS.

I'LL TRY TO KEEP A CLOSED MIND.

HOW WAS THE SEMINAR?

THE GUY HAD SOME INTERESTING IDEAS ABOUT THE FUTURE OF OFFICE DESIGN. FOR EXAMPLE, HE SAYS EMPLOYEES ARE MOST EFFICIENT IN AN OFFICE SETTING THAT'S MORE LIKE THEIR HOME.

I'M THINKING OF BRINGING IN A LAUNDRY BASKET AND A SINK FULL OF DISHES.

SO, WHAT KIND OF BONEHEAD IDEAS WERE THEY TRYING TO PEDDLE AT THAT SEMINAR?

ACTUALLY IT WAS INTERESTING, RALPH. THEY TALKED ABOUT HOW OFFICES IN THE FUTURE MAY BE NON-TERRITORIAL, FOR EXAMPLE.

WHAT THE HECK DOES THAT MEAN?

EMPLOYEES WOULD SHARE A COMMON SPACE AND WOULDN'T HAVE DESKS TO CALL THEIR OWN.

OH YEAH, AND WHAT SORT OF ARMY ARE THEY PLANNING TO SEND TO TRY TO TAKE MY DESK AWAY?

WE DIDN'T GET INTO SPECIFIC BATTLE STRATEGIES.

29

HEY, DAD, CAN I GO TO CAMP THIS SUMMER?

UM, LET ME THINK ABOUT IT AND DISCUSS IT WITH YOUR MOM.

MOM, CAN I GO TO CAMP?

UM, LET ME THINK ABOUT IT AND DISCUSS IT WITH YOUR DAD.

IT'S LIKE DEALING WITH THE HOUSE AND THE SENATE... AND I'VE GOT ABOUT THE SAME CHANCE OF GETTING SOME ACTION.

I'M SORRY, HILARY, BUT DAD AND I AREN'T GOING TO SPEND MONEY TO SEND YOU TO SOMETHING CALLED NINTENDO CAMP.

AW, MOM.

DON'T YOU HAVE A BROCHURE FROM A CAMP THAT TEACHES YOU ABOUT NATURE?

THEY DON'T HAVE CAMPS LIKE THAT ANYMORE.

WHAT ABOUT THIS ONE? "CAMP FRIENDLY FOREST."

HOW DID THAT TREE-HUGGER THING GET IN HERE? AND WHERE'S THE ONE FROM THE ROCK VIDEO CAMP?

AM I A TOMBOY?

NO, YOU'RE A GIRL. "TOMBOY" IS AN OLD SEXIST WORD THAT ASSUMES BOYS ARE SUPPOSED TO BEHAVE ONE WAY AND GIRLS ANOTHER.

JASON CALLED ME A TOMBOY.

WHAT DID YOU DO?

I PUT HIM IN A HAMMERLOCK UNTIL HE TOOK IT BACK.

SEE, BOYS AREN'T THE ONLY ONES WHO RECOGNIZE THE UTILITY OF AN OCCASIONAL HAMMERLOCK.

IF A TOMBOY IS A GIRL WHO BEHAVES LIKE A BOY, WHAT'S A BOY WHO BEHAVES LIKE A GIRL?

A HENGIRL.

REALLY?

NO, I MADE THAT UP. THE WORD PEOPLE HAVED USED IS "SISSY."

SISSY? BEHAVING LIKE A GIRL MAKES YOU A SISSY? COUNT ME OUT.

SEE HOW SILLY STEREOTYPES ARE.

DO YOU LIKE BEING A GIRL?

ARE YOU THINKING MAYBE BEING A BOY IS EASIER?

MAYBE.

I'LL BET BEING A BOY ISN'T AS EASY AS IT LOOKS. WHAT IF YOU JUST WANTED TO BE A PLEASANT YOUNG PERSON, BUT SOCIETY EXPECTED YOU TO BE AN AGGRESSIVE LITTLE TWERP?

I NEVER THOUGHT OF THAT.

THINK OF THE PRESSURE.

* SALLY'S TREE FORT MET ALL CODE AND SAFETY REGULATIONS. NO NEED TO WRITE.

36

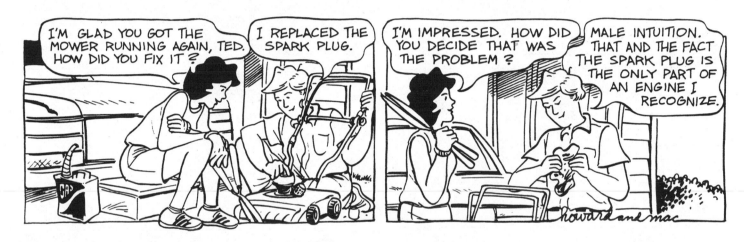

45

MEN REALLY TAKE A BEATING IN EVERY HUMOR SHOW ON THE TUBE, SAL. IT'S A STEADY BARRAGE OF JOKES ABOUT HAPLESS MALES.

ALL OTHER GROUPS ARE NOW ON THE TABOO LIST, TED. YOU'RE THE LAST GROUP WE CAN MAKE FUN OF WITHOUT FEAR OF BEING POLITICALLY INCORRECT. IF WE CAN'T MAKE MEN THE BUTT OF JOKES, COMEDY WILL DIE.

THE FATE OF WESTERN HUMOR RESTS ON MY BUTT?

AL BUNDY COULDN'T HAVE SAID IT BETTER.

I DON'T MIND A GOOD RIBBING, SAL, BUT IT SEEMS AS IF THE WHOLE TREND IN COMEDY IS TO MAKE MEN THE BUTT OF THE JOKES.

EVERYONE ELSE IS ON THE PROTECTED-GROUP LIST... ETHNIC GROUPS, RACIAL MINORITIES, RELIGIOUS GROUPS... IT'S EVEN GETTING HARD TO JOKE ABOUT WOMEN. YOU MALE WASPS ARE THE LAST GROUP WE CAN RIDICULE.

YOU'RE SAVING COMEDY, TED. YOU SHOULD BE PROUD.

IT'S SORT OF LIKE BEING RIDDEN OUT OF TOWN ON A RAIL... IF IT WEREN'T FOR THE HONOR OF THE THING, I'D RATHER WALK.

IT'S NOT FAIR, SAL. THE HUMOR BUSINESS MAKES US MEN THE BUTT OF EVERY JOKE BECAUSE THEY THINK WE'RE THE LAST SAFE TARGET.

YOU'RE EXAGGERATING, TED. MEN AREN'T THE ONLY GROUP IT'S SAFE TO POKE FUN AT.

OH, SURE, LUMP US IN WITH LAWYERS AND POLITICIANS. YOU REALLY KNOW HOW TO HURT A GUY.

YOU FORGOT TV EVANGELISTS.

52

60

61

DAD SAID YOU'RE RUNNING LATE, SO HE MADE MY LUNCH.

WHAT A GUY.

HE'S A GOOD PACKER. GUESS HOW MANY DOUGHNUTS FIT IN THIS BAG.

LET ME SEE THAT.

DAD'LL BE HURT THAT YOU ACTUALLY BELIEVED HE PACKED ME A DOUGHNUT LUNCH.

NOT IF SOME LITTLE TROUBLEMAKER DOESN'T TELL HIM.

AH, IT'S THE CHAUVINIST. I HEAR YOU THINK MEN AREN'T CAPABLE OF PACKING GOOD LUNCHES FOR THEIR KIDS.

I DIDN'T SAY THAT. HILARY TOLD ME YOU MADE HER LUNCH AND IMPLIED IT WAS ALL DOUGHNUTS.

AND YOU BELIEVED HER.

WELL, SORT OF.

OINK, OINK.

TODAY'S OFF TO A FLYING START. ALREADY I'VE GOT MY DAUGHTER GETTING ME INTO TROUBLE AND MY HUSBAND OINKING AT ME.

70

SALLY FORTH by Greg Howard

TELL ME IF MY VOICE SOUNDS GRATING ENOUGH.

WHAT ARE YOU DOING?

PUTTING A NEW MESSAGE ON OUR ANSWERING MACHINE.

THANK YOU FOR CALLING THE FORTH HOUSEHOLD. IF YOU HAVE A TOUCH-TONE PHONE, PRESS 1.

IF YOU WISH TO LEAVE A MESSAGE FOR HILARY, PRESS 2.

IF YOU WISH TO LEAVE A MESSAGE FOR A NON-HILARY, PRESS 3 FOR SALLY OR 4 FOR TED.

IF YOU ARE CALLING TO INTERRUPT OUR DINNER WITH A SALES PITCH, PRESS 5.

IF YOU WISH TO HAVE THESE OPTIONS REPEATED, PRESS 6.

IF YOU WISH TO SPEAK TO A HUMAN BEING, PRESS ANY NUMBER YOU WANT BECAUSE IT WON'T DO ANY GOOD. THE WHOLE REASON FOR VOICE MAIL IS THAT WE DON'T WANT TO TALK TO YOU.

HAVE A NASTY RUN-IN WITH VOICE MAIL AGAIN TODAY?

IF YOU CAN'T BEAT 'EM, JOIN 'EM.

I JUST REMEMBERED I NEED SHOES TO GO WITH THAT BLUE OUTFIT I HAVE, TED. DO YOU MIND IF WE LOOK AS LONG AS WE'RE OUT HERE? IT'LL ONLY TAKE A MINUTE.

OKAY.

WHAT A PAIR. INCREDIBLE AS IT SOUNDS, SHE ACTUALLY BELIEVES IT'LL ONLY TAKE A MINUTE. AND WHAT ABOUT HIM? MR. GULLIBLE HAS BOUGHT HIMSELF ANOTHER SECTION OF THE BROOKLYN BRIDGE.

I THOUGHT YOU SAID IT WOULD ONLY TAKE A MINUTE. IT'S ALREADY BEEN 10.

IT DIDN'T SEEM THIS BUSY WHEN WE CAME IN.

A CLERK HASN'T EVEN TALKED TO US YET.

THIS ALWAYS HAPPENS TO ME. STORE CLERKS THINK I'M ALREADY BEING HELPED.

WELL QUIT LOOKING SO DARN CONTENTED.

HOW'S THIS?

I'M NOT SURE THESE ARE THE RIGHT HUE. DO THEY HAVE A TOUCH OF INDIGO IN THEM? I'M PRETTY SURE MY OUTFIT IS A BLUER BLUE.

WHAT DO **YOU** THINK, TED?

ME? BUT I WAS JUST SITTING HERE MINDING MY OWN BUSINESS.

ANOTHER HAPLESS MALE GETS SUCKED INTO THE "COLOR" VORTEX.

THE CRIMINALS WALK AROUND OUTSIDE, AND WE GET LOCKED UP IN HERE? WHO THOUGHT UP THIS SYSTEM?

DID YOU CHECK IF THE DOORS ARE DEADBOLTED?

I DID IT LAST NIGHT. IT'S YOUR TURN.

BUT WHAT IF THERE'S A BAD GUY CROUCHED BY THE DOOR?

OH, ALL RIGHT. I'LL GO.

FEMINISM TAKES AN INTERESTING TWIST WHEN THERE'S A BAD GUY CROUCHED BY THE DOOR.

LET ME KNOW WHEN THERE'S A BAD WOMAN CROUCHED DOWN THERE, AND I'LL TAKE MY TURN.

I WISH THEY DIDN'T HAVE TO CALL THEM **DEAD**BOLTS.

"APPLIANCES THAT CAUSE TROUBLE,"
THE NEXT SALLY

OH, BY THE WAY, I FIXED THE BATHROOM SCALE.

I DIDN'T KNOW ANYTHING WAS WRONG WITH IT.

I WEIGH 170, BUT IT SAID I ONLY WEIGHED 167 SO I TURNED IT UP THREE POUNDS.

YOU KNOW THE MOST INCREDIBLE PART ABOUT THIS?

WHAT'S THAT?

YOU'RE ABOUT TO DIE, AND YOU DON'T EVEN REALIZE WHY.

C'MON, SAL, YOU MADE ME SPILL MY COFFEE.

MY BOOK SAYS COLUMBUS DISCOVERED AMERICA, BUT HOW COULD HE? THE INDIANS WHO WERE HERE WHEN HE ARRIVED DISCOVERED IT WAY BEFORE COLUMBUS DID.

HE CALLED THEM INDIANS, BUT HE WASN'T IN INDIA SO HE SHOULD HAVE CALLED THEM AMERICANS. EXCEPT AMERICA WASN'T CALLED THAT UNTIL LATER WHEN AMERIGO VESPUCCI DECIDED TO NAME IT AFTER HIMSELF.

THIS IS VERY CONFUSING.

AND WE HAVEN'T EVEN TALKED ABOUT LEIF ERICSON YET.

HOW COME MY HISTORY BOOK SAYS COLUMBUS DISCOVERED AMERICA? IF PEOPLE WERE ALREADY LIVING HERE WHEN HE SAILED UP, THEY MUST HAVE DISCOVERED IT BEFORE HE DID.

SOMETIMES WE NEED TO TAKE A FRESH LOOK AT WHAT THE HISTORY BOOKS SAY.

THAT'S WHAT I TOLD MY TEACHER AFTER OUR LAST TEST.

DIDN'T WORK, DID IT?

MY TEACHER SAYS WE DON'T KNOW EXACTLY WHO DISCOVERED AMERICA. APPARENTLY THEY CAME ACROSS THE BERING STRAIT THOUSANDS OF YEARS AGO AND MIGRATED DOWN.

SHE SAYS THE FIRST ONE HERE WAS PROBABLY A WOMAN BECAUSE HER HUSBAND HAD TO GO BACK FOR THE TV CLICKER.

MY TEACHER THINKS HISTORY NEEDS A LITTLE SPICING UP.

MAYBE SHE'S RIGHT.

79

THE GOSPEL ACCORDING TO SALLY

"THOU SHALT NOT COVET THY NEIGHBOR'S HUSBAND." (BESIDES, WHY WOULD YOU WANT TO? CHANCES ARE HE HAS AT LEAST AS MANY ANNOYING LITTLE HABITS AS YOUR OWN HUSBAND.)

THE GOSPEL ACCORDING TO SALLY

"THE ROAD TO HELL IS PAVED WITH GOOD INTENTIONS. THE ROAD TO PROCRASTINATION IS PAVED WITH CHOCOLATE." (THE GOSPEL UNDERSTANDS HUMAN NATURE.)

THE GOSPEL ACCORDING TO SALLY

"DO UNTO OTHERS AS YOU WOULD HAVE THEM DO UNTO YOU." (THIS APPLIES EVERYWHERE EXCEPT EMPLOYEE LOUNGES WHERE THE RULE SEEMS TO BE "TO HECK WITH THE REST OF 'EM.")

THE GOSPEL ACCORDING TO SALLY

"Am I my brother's keeper?" (Only until you get married and move away from home. Then you're your husband's keeper.)

THE GOSPEL ACCORDING TO SALLY

"Many are called, but few are chosen." (Actually, only the first part applies to those between the ages of 8 and 18.)

THE GOSPEL ACCORDING TO SALLY

"The meek shall inherit the earth." (The aggressive, however, shall inherit the closest parking spots.)

88

HOW MANY FROM YOUR FAMILY ARE COMING FOR THANKSGIVING, TED?

MY DAD SAID PROBABLY THREE BUT POSSIBLY UP TO EIGHT.

HOW CAN I PLAN WITHOUT AN EXACT NUMBER?

CAN'T WE JUST THROW ON SOME EXTRA PLATES?

LET ME TRY TO PUT THIS IN GUY TERMS. LET'S SAY YOU WERE EXPECTING THREE OTHER PLAYERS FOR GOLF, AND EIGHT SHOWED UP...

I SEE WHAT YOU MEAN.

CALL YOUR MOM AND ASK WHICH OF YOUR RELATIVES ARE COMING HERE FOR THANKSGIVING AND WHAT FOODS THEY'RE BRINGING.

MAYBE YOU SHOULD CALL HER. I MIGHT MESS IT UP.

I HAVE CONFIDENCE IN YOU, TED. YOU WON'T MESS IT UP.

BESIDES, I KNOW WHAT WILL HAPPEN TO YOU IF YOU DO.

YOU HAVE A WAY OF GETTING ME FOCUSED ON A TASK.

I GUESS MY UNCLE HUBERT WILL BE JOINING US FOR THANKSGIVING AFTER ALL. HE SAID NOT TO WORRY ABOUT GETTING CHEESE PUFFS FOR DURING THE FOOTBALL GAME BECAUSE HE'S BRINGING TWO BAGS.

SCRATCH THAT OFF MY LIST OF THINGS TO DO, WILL YOU? IT WAS RIGHT AT THE TOP.

HOW MANY TIMES DO YOU WANT ME TO APOLOGIZE FOR UNCLE HUBERT?

I'LL LET YOU KNOW WHEN YOU CAN STOP.

MOM, I CAN'T GET TO SLEEP! WHAT THE HECK ARE SUGAR PLUMS?

SALLY, TED AND HILARY HAVE CHRISTMAS DAY OFF. THE ONLY FAMILY MEMBER WHO DOESN'T IS THEIR CAT.

IT'S UP TO YOU. DO SOMETHING FUNNY.

EVEN IN COMIC STRIPS CATS WON'T DO WHAT YOU TELL THEM. HAPPY HOLIDAYS.

IS BEING A DICTATOR SOMETHING YOU LEARN OR IS IT A HEREDITARY DEAL?

KEEP WRITING.

OKAY, BUT IF IT'S HEREDITARY, MY KIDS WILL KNOW WHERE I GOT IT.

YOU CAN GO PLAY AS SOON AS YOU'RE DONE WRITING YOUR THANK-YOU NOTES.

DO YOU EVER FEEL LIKE YOU GET TAKEN FOR GRANTED AT WORK, TED?

IS RALPH TAKING YOU FOR GRANTED AGAIN?

IT'S NOT LIKE I NEED TO BE PATTED ON THE BACK FOR EVERY LITTLE THING... I'M A BIG GIRL... BUT EVEN SO, IT'D BE NICE TO HEAR "GOOD JOB, SAL" EVERY ONCE IN A WHILE.

LIKE MAYBE EVERY TWO OR THREE YEARS.

GOOD JOB, SAL.

YOU KNOW ME, TED, I'M NOT ONE OF THE WHINERS AT WORK. I DO MY JOB AND DON'T EXPECT TO BE CONSTANTLY PATTED ON THE BACK.

I KNOW, BUT EVEN SECURE PEOPLE NEED TO HEAR "NICE JOB" EVERY NOW AND THEN.

EXACTLY. THE CLOSEST RALPH GOT WAS A YEAR AGO WHEN HE SAID, "THIS ISN'T AS BAD AS SOME OTHER CRUD YOU'VE DONE."

AND YOU NEED MORE THAN THAT? I'M SURPRISED AT YOU, SAL.

AM I BEING OVERLY SENSITIVE, TED?

NOT AT ALL. EVEN SECURE PEOPLE LIKE YOU NEED AN OCCASIONAL PAT ON THE BACK AT WORK.

RALPH HAS A HARD TIME GIVING COMPLIMENTS.

HE DOESN'T SEEM TO HAVE A HARD TIME GIVING CRITICISM.

YOU HAVE TO REMEMBER HE'S A GRADUATE OF THE CRO-MAGNON SCHOOL OF MANAGEMENT.

I KNOW. I WORK FOR ONE OF HIS FRATERNITY BROTHERS.

121